A Wife and Mother

I Talk You Talk Press

CONTENTS

I Talk You Talk Press

CHAPTER ONE

It was a beautiful summer's day. Rhonda and Libby were sitting on a park bench watching the children play.

"Who are those children Anders and Rebecca are playing with?" asked Rhonda.

"The girl is Marcia," answered Libby. "She's in the same class as Rebecca at school. I don't know the name of the little boy. I've seen him with his father when he picks Marcia up from school. I guess he hasn't started school yet. So he must be younger than Anders."

"They're very young to be here alone," said Rhonda.

"They're not alone. That's their father standing near the swings. He's making sure the little boy doesn't fall off."

Rhonda stared at the tall red-haired man. "He keeps looking at you," she laughed. "I think he likes you!"

Libby pulled her sunhat down over her face. "He can look if he wants," she said. "I'm very happy with my husband, thank you! I don't need another man in my life!"

Rhonda sighed. She looked at Libby. Her blonde hair was long and shiny. She was wearing a pink T-shirt and straight blue jeans.

She's beautiful, she thought. *She's so tall and elegant, and she's such a nice person. My brother Kris was lucky to marry her. I'm short and dark and a bit overweight. No man in the park would look at me.*

Libby heard Rhonda sigh. She turned to her sister-in-law and patted her hand. "Are you OK?" she asked. "You have had such a hard time."

"Some days are harder than others," said Rhonda. "But I feel much better staying with you and Kris. You are so kind to let me stay with you for a few days. I couldn't have come to the music festival if I had to stay in a hotel."

"I think it's terrible that you got no money from the divorce. I can't believe that Barton got all the money, the house and the car. It wasn't fair."

"No," said Rhonda. "It wasn't fair. Never marry a lawyer! They are too smart when it comes to their own divorces! He made sure that he got everything and I got nothing."

"Kris and I worry about you," said Libby softly.

"I know, but it's OK. I never worked after I got married. I was so busy playing the oboe in the amateur orchestra and being the perfect lawyer's wife. But I've started my little business buying handcrafts made by women in Afghanistan and selling them here in the US. It's slow, but I'm doing OK."

"Well, we love having you stay with us. The children love having you stay too. You must stay with us as long as you want."

Rhonda smiled at Libby. "Thank you, but I'm fine. Salma is a lovely town, and I love to visit here. I'll go back to Wilmington tomorrow. I have my little apartment, and I have a lot of work to do with my new business."

They could hear Anders shouting, "Mom! Mom! Look what I can do!"

"Oh no!" laughed Libby. "He's climbing up the slide the wrong way! Does he think he's Superman?"

She jumped up, and hurried over to her son.

Rhonda sat and watched them. *Libby and Kris are so much in love. They have two beautiful children and a nice house. They are so lucky! The perfect marriage and the perfect family,* she thought. *What do I have? No husband, no children, a tiny apartment in a bad neighbourhood and a very old car.*

She wanted to cry but then she said to herself, *Think positive! You have a wonderful brother and sister-in-law. You have a great niece and nephew. You still have your music, and you won't play well in the concert tonight if you are miserable!*

She forced herself to smile when Libby came back to the bench with Rebecca and Anders.

"Did you have a nice time with your friends?" she asked the children.

"Yes," said Rebecca. "Marcia is in my class at school. She's taller than me, but I can swing higher!"

"It's time to go home," said Libby. "Anders is getting tired, and Aunty Rhonda has to get ready for her concert tonight."

They drove back to Kris and Libby's house. It was a normal family home in a good neighbourhood. But it was nicer than other houses in the street.

The windows were so clean that they sparkled. The paintwork of the house was perfect, and the garden was special. At the front of the house Libby grew roses and azaleas. Behind the house was a large vegetable garden.

"How do you find enough time to look after Rebecca and Anders and have such a beautiful garden?" asked Rhonda.

"The garden is my hobby," said Libby. "And I'm lucky. Kris earns enough money, so I don't have to work. I can be a fulltime mother. And I can help out at the school too."

"Doesn't Kris help you in the house and garden?"

Libby laughed. "He is not very good at work in the house. I don't think he knows how to use a paintbrush or a screwdriver. But it's OK. He is so busy with his students at the high school. And he is a wonderful husband and father."

The inside of the house was special too. Libby bought old furniture and repaired it. She made curtains and cushions and patchwork quilts. Everything was so clean and bright. It was the perfect family home.

She is so talented, thought Rhonda. *I love this house.*

Libby made a meal for the children. "Go and get ready for your concert," she said to Rhonda. "I'm so sorry. I want to come and hear you play. But Kris is away with the high school band and we don't like to use babysitters."

"It's OK," said Rhonda. "The event managers will make a video of the concert. You and Kris can watch that."

When Rhonda came back to the kitchen dressed in her long black dress for the concert, Libby was talking to Kris on the phone. She was smiling. "Yes, everything is OK here. The children have eaten, and Rhonda will leave for her concert soon," she said.

"How is Augusta?

"Is the band doing well in the competition?

"They are through to the semi-finals! That's wonderful!

"No. I'm not going to Rhonda's concert, but we can watch the video together when you come home. We love having her here. I wish she could stay, but she says she must go back to Wilmington tomorrow.

"We miss you. We'll see you on Wednesday. I love you!"

Libby hung up and turned to Rhonda. "I hate it when Kris is away. I miss him so much!"

She pointed to the table. "I know you don't like to eat too much before a concert. So I made some sandwiches."

Rhonda looked at the table. There was a plate of small sandwiches, and a jug of iced tea.

"That's perfect," she said.

Libby smiled. "I'll have some more food ready for you when you come back from the concert. I'm sure you'll be hungry then."

CHAPTER TWO

The children were tired. Libby bathed them and put them to bed early. "School tomorrow," she said.

"When's Daddy coming back?" asked Rebecca.

"Soon," answered Libby.

"How soon?" asked Anders.

"Well today is Sunday. He'll be back on Wednesday night. That's three days."

"I want him to come back sooner," said Anders. "I want him to play baseball with me."

"I'll play baseball with you tomorrow afternoon," said Libby.

"No!" shouted Anders. "You're no good at baseball! I want to play with Daddy."

Libby laughed. "I'm sorry. How about I read to you and Rebecca for a while?"

Rebecca was eight, and could read well, but she liked to listen when Libby read bedtime stories to Anders.

"What book would you like?"

"Big Dog and Little Dog!" shouted Anders. It was his favourite book.

"No!" shouted Rebecca. "You always want that. I want Mom to read a Tree House book."

Libby kissed Anders. "I'll read a Tree House book tonight, and I promise I'll read Big Dog and Little Dog to you tomorrow night."

Libby sat on the end of Anders' bed and read to the children. Then she kissed Anders again. He was already asleep.

She took Rebecca to her room and helped her into bed. "Good night," she said quietly. "Sleep well."

"Good night, Mom," said Rebecca sleepily.

Libby went back to the kitchen. She made a quiche and salad and put a bottle of white wine in the fridge. She set two places at the dining room table. *Rhonda and I can eat together when she comes back,* she thought.

She cleaned and tidied the kitchen. Then she tidied the children's toys in the living room. Back in the kitchen she checked a list on the fridge door.

Rebecca has swimming at school tomorrow. I must pack her swimsuit and towel. Then I have gardening club in the morning. I promised our president to take cookies to have with our coffee. Gardening club starts at 10:00am, so I'll have time to make them after I take the children to school. Then I'm helping with Anders' reading class in the afternoon. Another busy day!

She looked around the kitchen. *Oh! I forgot to take the garbage out!*

She took the plastic bag from the garbage container and put in a new plastic bag. She walked out the back door of the house to the end of the vegetable garden where there was a large garbage bin.

It was dark outside, but she had left the backdoor open. There was enough light from the kitchen for her to see.

As she came back to the house, she saw a piece of paper stuck to the back door. She took it into the house and read it. There were two words written on the piece of paper.

Libby's face went white. She leant against the table as though she had no strength in her legs to stand up.

After a short while, she stood up straight. She found the lighter Kris used for lighting the barbeque, and burnt the piece of paper in the kitchen sink. She ran water until all the ashes had washed away.

She walked to the bedroom she shared with Kris. She took her jewellery box from a drawer and opened it. In the bottom of the box was an old-fashioned locket with a photograph inside. She took a nail file and removed the photograph. There was a small piece of paper under the locket. It had a telephone number on it. She took the paper, replaced the photograph in the locket and put the locket back in the box. She put the box back in the drawer.

Then she took all her shoes out of the closet and pulled up a floorboard. Under the floorboard was a mobile phone.

Libby took the phone, replaced the floorboard and her shoes and went back to the kitchen. She put the phone number and the phone on the table and stared at them.

She sighed. She used the phone to call a number. A man answered. Libby said nothing, but the man spoke. "Midnight. The corner of Exchange and Crown streets."

Libby put the phone in a pocket of her jeans. She washed the tiny piece of paper down the sink.

Then Libby started working. She went to the children's bedrooms. They were sleeping deeply. She put the children's clothes for school the next day on the end of their beds.

She went through the house and picked up all the clothes and towels that needed washing. She went to the laundry and put everything in the washing machine. She packed Rebecca's swimwear into her sports bag. She made two school lunches and put them in the fridge.

When the washing machine finished its cycle, she put the washing in the dryer. She made the cookies for the gardening club. She folded laundry from the dryer and put it away.

It was getting late, but Libby was still working. She moved like a robot, doing household tasks. Finally, she stopped.

She went to her children's bedrooms. Anders' bed covers were on the floor. She picked them up and covered him. She kissed her children. She stood at the door and looked at them for a long time.

Then she went to her bedroom. She took off her wedding ring and put it under the pillow on Kris' side of the bed. Then she walked outside.

Libby stood behind a tree in the garden. She waited and watched. She saw Rhonda's car in the street. Rhonda drove the car into the driveway of the house. Libby saw Rhonda open the front door.

Then she stayed in the shadows as she walked down the street and away from the home she had shared with Kris, Rebecca and Anders.

Rhonda came into the house. She was excited. "Libby!" she called. "The concert went so well! I played better than I expected."

There was no answer.

Rhonda went into the kitchen. There was a note on the table.

---Hope the concert went well. Quiche is on the bench. Twenty minutes at 150 degrees in the oven. Wine and salad in fridge.---

Libby has gone to bed, thought Rhonda. *I'm not surprised. She works so hard.*

Then she saw a tray of cookies on a rack. There was another note.

—Cookies for gardening club meeting. Deliver to Wilma Lennon's house, 144 Salisbury Drive before 9:30am tomorrow morning.---

Rhonda laughed. *I think Libby is perfect. But she has to write herself reminder memos!*

Rhonda heated the quiche and enjoyed her meal with a glass of wine.

Then she went to bed. She was very quiet because she didn't want to wake Libby or the children.

CHAPTER THREE

The next morning, Rhonda woke up because Rebecca was standing next to her pillow.

"Where's Mommy?"

Rhonda climbed out of bed. "I guess she's sleeping," she said.

"No!" shouted Rebecca. "She's not in her bed. I looked."

Rhonda put on her robe and a pair of sandals. "Maybe she's in the garden. I'll go and look. Why don't you go and wake Anders up?"

Rhonda hurried out into the garden. There was no one there. She looked in the garage. Kris and Libby's car was there.

Back in the kitchen, Rebecca was trying to pour a glass of milk for Anders. Rebecca's face was red and shiny. She had been crying.

Anders was still sleepy. "Mommy pours milk better than you," he said to Rebecca.

Rebecca looked at Rhonda. "He doesn't understand that Mommy's not here," she said. "Mommy's always here. But today she's not."

Rhonda's heart melted. She hugged Rebecca. "It's OK," she said. "Don't worry. She'll be back soon."

I don't know what to do, thought Rhonda. *This is crazy. Where is she?* She looked at the two children. *Rebecca is frightened. When Anders realises Libby is not here, he will be frightened too. I must pretend that everything is normal.*

"Today's a special day!" she said brightly. "I don't have my own children. So your Mommy said I could be your mother this morning!"

Rhonda made breakfast. She looked in the refrigerator and found the school lunches.

"What clothes do you wear to school?" she asked Rebecca.

"There are clothes at the end of our beds," she said. "And I have swimming today."

Rhonda raced around the house. She found the school bags and the sports bag. She helped Anders to dress for school. She told the children to clean their teeth. She pulled on a T-shirt and jeans and drove the children to school.

When she got back from the school, she sat down at the kitchen table. *I'm so tired. I haven't had a cup of coffee. I haven't had a shower and I haven't had breakfast! How does Libby do this every day?*

Then she thought, *I've been so busy doing normal mother morning jobs, I haven't thought about Libby at all! Where is she?*

Rhonda walked through the house. Everything was very tidy. She opened the door to Kris and Libby's bedroom. The curtains were closed and the bed was made. *Did she leave very early this morning? I don't know what to do,* she thought.

She made coffee and toast for herself. She showered and dressed and took the cookies to Wilma Lennon's house. "Isn't Libby coming today?" asked Wilma.

"No. She can't come today," answered Rhonda.

"That's a pity," said Wilma. "She never misses our meetings. But thank you for the cookies. I'll bring the plate back to Libby tomorrow."

Rhonda drove back to the quiet house. *This is crazy! Libby would never do anything like this. Why didn't she call me, or text me? Maybe she left me a note and I didn't see it.*

She searched everywhere but she couldn't find a note. She looked in strange places like under the pillow in her bedroom and the drawers in the kitchen.

She went into Kris and Libby's bedroom.

Oh no! Rhonda was suddenly very frightened because Libby's phone was on the bed. *She would never leave the house without her phone! Someone has taken her! Keep calm! Keep calm! Don't panic. Shall I call the police? No! I'll call Kris. But I don't know what to say!*

She sat at the kitchen table. Her hands were shaking. She called Kris' number. He didn't answer. She left a voice message. "Call me as soon as possible."

Then she sent Kris a text with the same message. Time passed very slowly. Rhonda walked up and down the kitchen. Finally her phone rang.

"Hi sis!" Kris sounded very cheerful. "Good to hear from you. How was the concert? Aren't you going back to Wilmington today? You said to call urgently. Do you have car troubles? That old car of yours is a nightmare!"

"No! No!" Rhonda found it hard to speak. "Kris! It's Libby! She's disappeared!"

"Rhonda! I'm busy with the students here at band contest. I should be helping them to practice right now! Don't waste my time with jokes."

Rhonda thought Kris was going to hang up.

"Listen!" she shouted. "I didn't see Libby when I came home from the concert last night. I thought she was in bed. This morning she wasn't here, so I took the children to school. She wasn't here when I came back!"

"That's strange," said Kris slowly. "Libby doesn't do things like that. But I'm sure there's a simple explanation. Maybe she forgot to get plants for the gardening club. Or maybe she's helping at the school. Don't worry."

Rhonda's voice was shaking. "But Kris," she said. "The car is in the garage. And her phone is here. She went out without her phone!"

There was a long silence at the other end of the phone.

"Call the police," said Kris. "I'm coming back. It will take me four hours to drive home. Don't wait. Call the police now!"

CHAPTER FOUR

Rhonda called the police. "I want to report a missing person," she said.

"One moment please," said the police receptionist. "I'll transfer your call."

"Good morning, this is Police Officer Williams. How can I help you?"

"I want to report a missing person," said Rhonda.

"Your name and address please."

"My name is Rhonda Blake. I live in Wilmington."

"And your address?"

"Apartment 42d, Fitzbolton Street, but I'm staying with my brother and sister-in-law here in Salma. The address is 152 Marlborough Avenue."

"The missing person. Who do you want to report missing?" asked Officer Williams.

"My sister-in-law, Libby. She's not here. Everything is wrong. Something has happened to her!"

"What is your sister-in-law's full name and age?" he asked.

"Mrs Elizabeth Anne Blake. Everyone calls her Libby. She's thirty-two years old. You have to come and find her!" Rhonda's voice was shaking.

"When did you last see Mrs Blake?"

"I saw her at about six forty-five last night. I went out to play in a concert. Everything was quiet when I got back. I went to bed, and this morning she wasn't here."

"Are there any signs of a break-in or violence in the house?"

"No."

"I'm sorry, Ms Blake. You have reported Mrs Blake missing. People are reported missing all the time, but usually they appear again. You say there is no sign of a break-in or violence. She is an adult. We usually don't investigate missing adults until they have been missing for twenty-four hours or more."

"But she left her phone behind!" shouted Rhonda.

Officer Williams laughed. "I guess she forgot to take it. My sister does that all the time. Does Mrs Blake have a husband?"

"Yes. I called him. He can't understand it. He's away with the high school band, but he's coming back now."

"Don't worry. I'm sure there's a simple explanation. Please ask Mr Blake to call me when he gets back." He hung up.

Rhonda was very angry. *The policeman doesn't understand that this is serious. Maybe the house is a crime scene. I mustn't touch anything.*

She walked up and down the living room. Then she heard Libby's phone ringing. She ran into the bedroom and stared at it. She looked at the caller ID. It was someone called 'Angela'. *Shall I answer it? No! I mustn't touch anything.* She entered the caller's phone number into her own phone.

When Libby's phone stopped ringing, she called the number.

"Hello," said a woman's voice.

"Hello. Is this Angela?" asked Rhonda.

"Yes. Who is this?" said Angela.

"I'm Rhonda, Libby's sister-in-law."

"Hi, Rhonda. Libby told me you were coming to stay. How are you? I just called Libby, but she didn't answer. I guess she's busy."

"Libby's disappeared," said Rhonda. "Do you know where she is?"

"Disappeared? What do you mean?" asked Angela.

"I went out last night. When I came back the house was dark. I thought Libby had gone to bed.

"She was not in the house this morning. The children were here, but there was no sign of Libby!"

"Are the children all right?" asked Angela sharply.

"Yes. They are upset because their mother isn't here. But I took them to school. Kris is coming back from the band competition."

"It's very strange," said Angela. "Have you called the police?"

"Yes. But they say they can't do anything yet."

"Listen to me," said Angela. "I know you are worried and upset. I'm sure there is a simple answer. Please don't call people, or talk to the neighbours. This is a small town and people talk a lot."

"OK. I understand. Thank you for the advice," said Rhonda.

"One more thing," said Angela. "I'll be at the school to pick up my daughter at two thirty pm. If Libby isn't back by then, I guess you'll go to get the children from school. But why don't I take them back to my house for a play date? They often come here. Just tell Kris to call the school and say it's OK."

Rhonda made a coffee and sat in the garden. Finally, Kris parked outside the house in a school van. He ran towards the house.

He looked terrible. "Any news?" he shouted. "Is Libby back?"

"No. I'm sorry." Rhonda hugged her brother.

"What are the police doing?" Kris' face was red and shiny. *He looks like Rebecca looked this morning,* thought Rhonda.

Rhonda sighed. "I called them, but they said people go missing all the time. The house is normal, so they don't think anything bad has happened to her. But they said you should call them when you got back."

Kris ran into the house. Just then, a police car pulled up outside.

A police officer walked into the garden. "Are you Ms Blake?" he asked. "I'm Officer Damien Williams."

Rhonda felt very cold. "Do you have some news?' she asked.

Damien Williams' face was red. Damien looked embarrassed.

"No. No news. But I met my mother for an early lunch today. She had been at the gardening club this morning. Of course I didn't say anything about your call, but she was talking about Mrs Blake. She said it was strange that Mrs Blake wasn't at the club this morning. 'She never misses', she said. Then she talked about her a lot. My mother said, 'Libby should get a medal as wife and mother of the year'. I started thinking that maybe the situation is serious. So I jumped in the car and came here. Is Mr Blake back yet?"

"Yes, he's in the house," answered Rhonda. "So please go and talk to him."

Rhonda waited outside. Then Kris came into the garden and said, "Come in and help me. I can't make him understand."

The police officer was sitting at the table. He smiled. "Please call me Damien. May I call you Rhonda?"

Rhonda sat down. "Sure, that's fine."

"Please answer some questions," he said.

Damien asked Rhonda a lot of questions.

She told him everything that had happened. She told him about the cookies, and the lunch boxes. She told him that she saw Libby's phone in the bedroom.

Kris was walking up and down the kitchen. He was very angry and very impatient.

Finally he shouted, "Why are you asking all these stupid questions? Why aren't you out looking for my wife?"

Damien looked at his phone. Then he said, "Mr Blake. It's two o'clock. Shouldn't you go and get your children from school?"

"Libby's friend Angela said that she would take the children home to her house for a play date," said Rhonda. "Call the school Kris, and tell them it's OK for Rebecca and Anders to go with Angela."

"No! My wife is missing! I want to see my children. I want to know that they are safe. I want my children here in the house with me!"

"Kris!" Rhonda wanted her brother to understand. "It'll be better if the children go to Angela's house for a little while. It's not good for them to be here now."

"Why don't you go to the school, so you can see your children?" said Damien. "But I agree with Rhonda. It's a good idea for them to have a play date this afternoon. Angela will take them, and you can come back here."

"OK," said Kris angrily.

He wasn't happy, but he went out to the garage to get the car.

Rhonda was worried. "He is in a terrible state. I hope he'll be safe driving."

"I hope so too," said Damien. "But I wanted to talk to you alone. Do you think Mrs Blake had a boyfriend?"

"What!" Rhonda thought Damien was joking. "Of course not! Kris and Libby have the perfect marriage!"

Then she told Damien about the phone call from Kris the night before. "Libby said she loved Kris. She said 'I hate it when Kris is away. I miss him so much'."

"What do you think happened?" Damien asked Rhonda. "Why has your sister-in-law disappeared?"

Rhonda put her head in her hands. "I don't know," she whispered.

"I can't believe she left to be with another man. Kris looked at her phone. He looked at all the contact numbers. He checked all the calls and messages. He knew everyone she contacted. There was nothing strange.

"She seemed so happy. I can't believe she left because she didn't like her life. Was she kidnapped?"

Damien coughed. "But if she was kidnapped, surely there would be some signs in the house. A broken lock or window, signs of a struggle?"

"Maybe someone got in and drugged her," said Rhonda.

"I don't know," said Damien. "I'm sorry. But my sister makes school lunches in the morning. Mrs Blake made school lunches last night and left them in the refrigerator.

"And the cookies for the gardening club meeting today? OK. I understand that she might make them the night before. But why did she leave a note to say where to take them? I think she knew she was leaving."

Rhonda was very angry. "Maybe she thought she would forget where to take the cookies! And call her Libby! She is a real person!"

Damien stood up. "I'm sorry I upset you. I'll go back to the police station now and talk to my boss. Here is my card. Please call me if you think of anything, or if you find out something new."

He walked to the back door and turned around.

"And please take care of your brother. He's like a crazy person."

CHAPTER FIVE

Damien went back to the police station. He wrote up his report and went to talk to his boss. Police Captain Percy Lawrence was sitting in his office as usual.

He was a fat, red-faced man. Damien didn't like him. *He's so lazy. He loves his badge and his uniform. He loves talking to the media, he loves being on TV, but he doesn't do any work.*

Damien knocked on the office door.

"Can I talk to you, Boss?" he asked.

Percy took his feet off the desk. "Sure. Come on in. What's your problem? Kids breaking windows again?"

"No," said Damien. "It's a missing person. Here's my report. I'm worried."

"Is it a child?" Percy's eyes lit up.

He's thinking about being on TV, thought Damien. *It makes me tired.*

"No. It's a thirty-two year old housewife. She hasn't been seen since yesterday evening."

Damien told Percy everything he knew about Libby's disappearance.

Percy leant back in his chair and laughed.

"It's not twenty-four hours yet. Why worry?"

"It seems Mrs Blake is a very special person. Everyone thinks she is a very good wife and mother. She's not the kind of person to go away and leave everything," said Damien.

Percy laughed. "The families of missing persons always say that. It doesn't mean anything."

He put his hands over his big stomach. "I have been a policeman for a long time. I have experience. She has killed herself, or she has run away with another man."

"But, Boss," said Damien. "Maybe she was kidnapped."

Percy was angry. "Salma is my town! There are no kidnappings here!"

"What shall I do?" asked Damien.

"Nothing," said Percy.

"Mrs Blake is very popular and her husband is a teacher at the high school. Maybe a lot of people will talk."

Damien could see Percy's mind working. *He's thinking about bad publicity,* he thought.

"OK," said Percy after a few moments. "Find some people to look for her body. Tell them to look in the parks and along the river. I'll talk to the newspaper people."

Damien's mobile phone rang. He looked at the screen. "Can I take this call?" he asked. "It's Mrs Blake's sister-in-law."

Percy nodded.

Damien answered the call. Rhonda was almost screaming. "Kris was sure there must be a message from Libby. He searched their bedroom. Libby's wedding ring was under his pillow on the bed!"

"OK, Rhonda. I'll call you back in a few minutes." Damien told Percy about the wedding ring.

"See!" laughed Percy. "Forget about the search for her body. I was right. The wedding ring proves it. She's run away with another man."

Then he said, "It's a pity. The newspapers and television won't be interested in that story."

He's a really horrible man, thought Damien. *He doesn't care about anyone. But he's my boss. I have to do what he says.*

The situation back at the house was very difficult. Kris sat in the living room. He wouldn't talk to Rhonda. He kept on saying, "I don't believe it."

Rhonda went to pick up the children from Angela's house. When Angela saw the car in the driveway, she came out to talk to Rhonda.

"How are Anders and Rebecca?" asked Rhonda.

"They're very quiet, but I think they're OK. Anders doesn't understand anything, but Rebecca is feeling very bad."

"Thank you for your help," said Rhonda. "I'll take them home now."

Angela put her hand on Rhonda's arm. "No, wait. I have to talk to you first. I promised you I wouldn't say anything to anyone about Libby's disappearance. I promise you, I didn't. You must believe me. I didn't tell anyone. But I've already had three phone calls this afternoon. I told you what this town is like. Everyone is talking already."

"But how did they know?" asked Rhonda.

"First, Kris got your phone call at the motel where he was staying with the school band and the other teachers. He took one of the school's vans and drove away. A lot of the students saw him go. One of the other teachers on the trip told his wife about it on the phone. Then people saw the school van parked outside his house.

"Second, Rebecca asked her school teacher where her mother was. Other children heard her. They told their parents after school.

"So many stories are going around. I tried to tell people on the phone that there was no drama, but of course they didn't believe me."

"Angela," said Rhonda. "This is not your fault. You are a good friend to Libby. I'll take the children home now."

Rhonda took the children home and told them to play in their bedrooms. She looked in the refrigerator and freezer and found food to cook. *I'll have to go to the supermarket tomorrow,* she thought. Then she stopped. *What am I thinking? I don't think Libby is coming back!*

She went to find Kris. He wasn't in the living room. She found him sitting on Rebecca's bed. He was hugging his children tightly and crying.

The children looked very scared.

"Kris! No!" she whispered. "You're frightening the children."

She took Rebecca and Anders away from Kris, and took them into the back garden.

"I want carrots to cook for dinner," she said. "Please find some carrots for me."

"I don't like carrots," said Anders.

"That's OK," she answered. "I'm sure you're very clever. I'm sure you can find carrots. Maybe you can find some other vegetables too. Find something you want to eat."

"Peas!" shouted Anders and ran towards the vegetable garden.

Rebecca took Rhonda's hand. "I'm scared," she said.

"I know. But don't worry. Everything will be all right. Look after your little brother."

When she went back into the house, she heard the front doorbell ring.

There was a tall man standing at the door. He looked embarrassed. "Uh. Can I talk to Kris please?"

"Just a minute." Rhonda went to look for Kris. He was lying on Rebecca's bed crying. She went back to the door. "Sorry, Kris is busy right now. Can I give him a message?"

"I'm Lars Peterson. I work with Kris. He took one of the school vans from the competition. I'm sorry, but we need it back."

"Sure," said Rhonda. "But I don't know where the keys are."

"It's OK," answered Lars. "I looked. The keys are in the van. Can I take it please?"

"Sure," said Rhonda.

"Thanks." Lars turned to walk away, but then he turned back. "Kris and I are good friends. Is everything OK?"

"Everything is fine!" Rhonda shut the door.

She cooked a meal and fed the children. Kris wouldn't eat. She persuaded him to go to bed. *Should I call the doctor? He needs a sedative or something to help him sleep.*

She got everything ready for the children for school the next day, and sat with them reading stories until they finally fell asleep.

She was very tired. It was about 10:00pm when Damien knocked on the back door. He was wearing jeans and heavy boots. "Can I come in?" he asked. Rhonda stood back, and he walked into the house.

"Where's Mr Blake?" he asked.

"In his bedroom. I hope he's asleep. Do you want to talk to him?"

"No. Leave him. I wanted to tell you. You might hear people moving around and see torches. There will be a search party. They are looking for Libby."

"A police search?"

"No. My boss doesn't think it's necessary. The townspeople have organised a search party."

Rhonda looked at Damien's clothes. "And you are going with them?"

"Yes. I might lose my job, but I'm joining the search party."

"What are they looking for?"

"Maybe some sign that she was kidnapped. Or...," Damien stopped.

Rhonda felt very cold. She thought she might faint. She sat down suddenly.

"Or her body?"

"I'm sorry. But yes," said Damien gently.

"But why? Your boss thinks there's no problem, but the townspeople don't agree?"

"Everyone in this town knows all the facts. They know Libby prepared everything for today before she disappeared. They know about the cookies for the gardening club. They know she left her phone behind. And they know about the wedding ring."

Rhonda could not believe it. "What! Did you tell people?"

"No. Do you think I'm that kind of person?" Damien said angrily. "My boss left the police station around four o'clock this afternoon. He often leaves early. He went to his favourite bar. He drank a lot. He had a good story to tell. He told everyone in the bar about his stupid junior officer. He thought it was great joke that I was worried about a missing woman. That I thought she might be in trouble. He told them everything I put in my report. He told everyone it was very simple. He was smart, and he knew that Libby had run away with another man."

"But people didn't believe him?"

"Kris and Libby are popular. Many people know them, and they have different ideas. She had some kind of mental problem and lost her memory. She killed herself. She was kidnapped. She was murdered. And of course, some people like the story of the secret lover. Don't forget. My boss told the drinkers in the bar about her wedding ring."

He stood up. "I have to go. I hope I'll have some news for you tomorrow morning."

"But it might not be good news."

"I'm sorry," said Damien again. "It might not be good news."

"I understand. Thank you."

"Don't thank me. I want to do what's right."

CHAPTER SIX

Damien came back the next morning, and asked to talk to Kris and Rhonda together.

He told Kris about the search party.

Kris was very angry.

"Why didn't you tell me? I would have come with you."

"We had a lot of people," said Damien. "Teachers from the high school and parents. Everyone wanted to help. It was better that you got some sleep."

"Did you find anything?" asked Kris.

Rhonda held her breath.

"No. We looked everywhere in the town. We looked in the parks, the school grounds, in neighbours' gardens, and along the river. Everything was completely normal. There was no sign of your wife. There was no sign that she had been to any of those places. I'm sorry. There is nothing more I can do."

"You have to keep on looking!" Kris shouted.

"My boss thinks that Mrs Blake has left town. He thinks she left because she wanted to go. He says the police can't do anything."

Damien didn't want to say that his boss believed that Libby had left town with another man.

It will upset him too much, he thought. *But he'll find out soon enough. People will talk.*

"I have to go now," he said.

Damien got up and walked to the door. Rhonda walked with him.

"I'm sorry," he said.

Rhonda never forgot the next few weeks.

Kris would not leave the house. "Libby is coming back," he said. "I must be here when she comes."

Rhonda discovered that Kris was not good at looking after the children or running the house. He couldn't cook. He didn't know anything about laundry or housework.

"Libby does that," he said.

"I'll teach you," said Rhonda.

"No. Can't you stay for a while and help me? It will only be a few days. Libby will be back soon."

Rhonda was angry with her brother, but she understood. *He loved Libby so much,* she thought. *He can't believe she has gone.*

She gave up her apartment in Wilmington and moved into Kris and Libby's house. *I'm lucky that I run my little company from home,* she thought. *I can do everything from here.*

She cleaned the house and looked after the children. She shopped for food and cooked. Day after day, Kris sat in his bedroom staring at the walls. He ate very little, and wouldn't play with the children. Rhonda found it hard to find time to work on her business.

Rebecca and Anders missed their mother a lot. And they had a hard time at school.

Often, when Rhonda picked the children up from school, they were very unhappy. Anders was too young to understand the things that the other children said, but he knew something was very wrong.

Rebecca cried every night. "They say Daddy killed Mommy," she said. "They say Mommy hated her life and killed herself. Did Mommy hate me?"

Most mornings, the children didn't want to go to school.

Rhonda did her best to comfort the children, but it was very difficult. She also worried about Kris.

"You must go back to work," she said to him. "Sitting at home all day is not good." But he wouldn't listen to her.

One Sunday night, Lars, Kris' friend from the high school came to visit. He talked to Kris for a long time. Rhonda didn't know what Lars said, but the next day, Kris went back to his job at the high school.

Rhonda was pleased. *Things will get better now,* she thought.

For a few days, life was easier. Kris ate more. He sometimes played with the children.

Rhonda tried to find time to work in Libby's garden. It was looking terrible. There were weeds everywhere, and the grass was long.

She was working outside one afternoon, when a voice said, "Excuse me."

Rhonda was surprised. She looked up. The voice was coming from the other side of the fence.

"Excuse me," said the voice again. "I'm Felicia. I live here. Can I talk to you?"

"Sure," said Rhonda. "Would you like to come over here? I'll make coffee."

"Yes," said Felicia. "I have something important to tell you."

Rhonda went inside to make coffee. She soon saw an older woman with two sticks at the kitchen door. "Come in," she said. "Can I help you to get up the steps?"

"No, no. I'm fine," said Felicia.

She climbed the steps slowly and sat at the table.

Rhonda made the coffee and put the cups on the table. "I'm sorry," she said. "There are no cookies. I never seem to have enough time."

"That's OK," said Felicia. "I didn't come for cookies."

Rhonda sat down. She looked at Felicia. She had bright eyes and a kind face. "What did you want to tell me?"

"I have wanted to talk to you for a long time," said Felicia. "But I was worried. I thought you would think I was an old woman who liked to gossip. But I saw you in the garden today, and I thought I must talk to you."

"OK," answered Rhonda. She was wondering what Felicia wanted to say.

"I was a teacher at the elementary school until I got ill. I had to stop because I couldn't walk well. Some days I can't leave the house. But today is a good day. I can walk a little. Libby and I were good friends. I knew her well. Most days I sit in my living room. I can see this house and the street. I saw Libby every day. I know many people are saying Libby had a secret lover. But I know it is not true!"

"How do you know?"

"Because she had no time!"

Rhonda was surprised. "What do you mean?" she asked.

"I saw Libby take the children to school. I saw her work in the garden. I saw her go to help at the school and go to the gardening club, the tennis club, and her art classes.

"She was home every evening when Kris came back from work. If she went out at night, Kris and the children were with her. The weekends were the same. She was always with the children, and usually her husband as well. If you have a secret lover, you have to see them. You have to meet your lover! When did Libby have time to go out for romantic dinners with someone else?"

Rhonda was very interested in what Felicia was saying. *I didn't believe the story about the secret lover, but lately I have begun to wonder if it was true,* she thought.

"Uh, maybe she met someone online. You know there are dating services."

"But she didn't have a computer!" said Felicia.

"That's true," Rhonda was thinking hard. "Kris has a computer at work. And he has a laptop he brings home sometimes, but there was no computer in this house. My computer is here now. I use it for my business, but there wasn't a home computer before. What about the library? Libby could have used a computer there."

Felicia laughed. "In this town? Everyone would know if she went to the library to use a computer. And there would always be someone looking over her shoulder to see what she was doing! No. Libby didn't have a secret lover!"

"Then where is she? What happened?" asked Rhonda.

"I don't know," said Felicia. "But I also want to tell you there is another story in the town. Some people think that her husband killed her!"

"What!" Rhonda could not believe what she was hearing. "He was with the school band in Augusta! He was three or four hours' drive away!"

Felicia patted Rhonda's hand. "The students had a performance on the Sunday afternoon. That night they went to watch the performances of other schools, but Kris didn't go. He said he had a headache. He said he would call home, and then he would go to bed. No one saw him until the next morning.

"Some people are saying he had enough time to drive back here, kill Libby, hide her body and drive back to Augusta."

"That's crazy," shouted Rhonda. "If he came to the house I would have heard something. It's not true!"

"Of course it isn't true," said Felicia. "But I wanted you to know."

"Some children at school told Rebecca that Kris had killed her mother," said Rhonda slowly. "I thought it was silly children's talk. But the children heard it from their parents!"

"I'm sorry," said Felicia. "I don't believe Libby had a secret lover. And I don't believe Kris killed her. The gossip and the stories in this town are horrible, but they will stop. Something else will happen. They will find another scandal to talk about."

"Felicia, what happened to Libby?" asked Rhonda.

"I don't know. Maybe we will never know."

Felicia left, and Rhonda looked at the clock. "Oh no! I'll be late to pick up the children."

That evening when Kris came home from work, he looked terrible. He was very quiet. He sat at the table with the children, but he didn't eat.

After the children were in bed, he said to Rhonda, "I can't teach anymore."

"Why not? You love teaching."

"Yes I do. But I can't teach in a school where half the students think I was a hopeless husband, and the other half think I killed my wife!"

"Maybe you should move to another town. You could get a job in another high school. It would be good for Rebecca and Anders too. I could come with you."

"No!" shouted Kris. He banged the table. "I have to stay here! I have to wait for Libby to come back."

CHAPTER SEVEN

Kris went to work the next day as usual. He didn't say anything more about leaving his job, but Rhonda was very worried. *Everything is so bad,* she thought. *And the school holidays are coming. How can I run my business when the children are home all day? Kris will have to help. But will he?*

She was surprised to get a phone call from Damien Williams.

"Do you remember me?" he asked.

"Of course," said Rhonda.

"Uh. Could you meet me for coffee? I want to talk to you."

She was feeling tired. She didn't want to talk to a policeman. Then she remembered that Damien had gone out with the search party. He knew his boss would be angry with him, but he had gone anyway. He had said 'I want to do what's right'.

"Yes. OK."

"Great! I'll meet you at the coffee shop near the library."

Damien was waiting for Rhonda.

They ordered coffees. "Let's sit outside, away from other people," said Damien. "I don't want other people to hear us."

Oh no! thought Rhonda. *Someone has found Libby! She's dead!*

Damien was smiling. "Nobody in this town knows yet. But I'm going to have a new boss! My boss, Percy Whitehouse, went to Charleston for the weekend. He went out drinking with some old friends. He drank too much. Then he crashed his car. He is in big trouble with the police in Charleston. Of course, he'll lose his job with the police. I'm very pleased. He was so lazy.

"You know he stopped me investigating what happened to Libby.

And he never made a record that Libby had disappeared. The new guy is called Pete Sampson. He called the police station today and asked about the cases we had. I told him about Libby. I think he will let me do some work so we can find out what happened. I have some ideas I want to work on."

"What ideas?" asked Rhonda.

"First," said Damien, "I thought about Libby's family. No one asked about them. I thought maybe she went to stay with them. Or maybe her family would have some ideas."

"Sorry," said Rhonda. "Libby has no family."

"No family at all?" Damien was surprised.

"No brothers or sisters or parents," said Rhonda. "When Kris met her at university, she had no family. No one from her family came to their wedding. Our parents died in a car crash a few months after they married. I think that's why Libby and Kris were so close. They have no one else."

"Kris has you," said Damien gently.

"Yes. That's true."

"So there's no family I can contact." Damien looked disappointed.

"I don't know. Before Libby married Kris, her family name was Emmett. And I've remembered something else. Libby has an aunt. She lives in the Bahamas. She sends birthday and Christmas presents for the children."

"Do you have a name and address?"

"I'll look in the house. I'm sure I can find something."

"That would be great!"

Damien looked at his phone. "I have to go. Please don't say anything to Kris. I might not find anything. I don't want him to be disappointed. And please don't say anything about Percy! Everyone in this town will know tomorrow, but today it's a secret!"

He hurried away.

Rhonda went back to the house and searched. She felt bad about looking through Kris and Libby's private papers, but she thought it was important.

There were no letters or cards. There were no contacts in Libby's address book. Libby's phone was still in the bedroom she had shared with Kris. Rhonda charged it and looked at all the phone contacts. There was no number with the area code for the Bahamas. It was very strange.

Then she had an idea. *Rebecca had a birthday just before I came here. She got a big dolls house. She showed it to me. Kris said it was a present from Libby's aunt. I haven't done anything about recycling all the paper and cardboard in the garage. I've been too busy. I wonder if the doll's house box is still there.*

She hurried to the garage and searched through the pile of paper and cardboard waiting to go to the recycle centre.

She found the box. The present had been sent from a toyshop. *I guess that's not a lot of help,* she thought. *But maybe Damien can find out who ordered it.*

She ripped the label off the box. On her way to pick up the children from school, she stopped at the police station.

She asked to speak to Damien. "This was all I could find," she said. She gave him the label. "I don't know if it will help you."

"There was nothing else?" Damien was surprised.

"No," said Rhonda. "It's very strange."

The next day, everyone in Salma knew about Percy Whitehouse, his car crash, and the drink driving charges.

Everyone was talking about it. It was the big news in town. People did not talk about Libby so much, and life got easier.

A few days later, Damien called. "Can I meet you again?" he asked.

Rhonda met Damien at the coffee shop.

"Do you have news?"

Damien looked serious. "Yes I do. I contacted the toy shop. It was difficult, because I'm only a policeman from a small town. But I found out something.

"The toy shop knows Rebecca's and Anders' birthdays. So they have their ages. They have an order to send a suitable present for their birthdays and every Christmas."

"But the aunt! Does she pay for the presents?" Rhonda was amazed.

"I don't know," said Damien slowly. "The toy shop wouldn't tell me who made the order, or who pays. But the toy shop manager told me the order and the payment come from New York!"

"I can't tell Kris," said Rhonda.

"No. You mustn't tell Kris. He will be worried. I told my boss. He's a really good guy. He is very angry that Percy didn't look for Libby. He has a friend in the FBI. He plans to ask her for help. I'll tell you when I have more news."

CHAPTER EIGHT

Kris got a phone call from the police station. The new police boss, Pete Sampson, wanted to talk to him.

"Mr Blake, can you come to the police station sometime this afternoon?"

"Do you have news of my wife?" asked Kris. He was very excited.

"I have some information," answered Pete Sampson. "But I don't want to talk on the phone."

"OK," said Kris. "I can leave school early. I can come about four o'clock. Is that OK?"

"Yes. I'll see you then."

It was the last day before the school holidays, and Libby's friend Angela had arranged a party. Rhonda took Rebecca and Anders to Angela's house.

All the children had a great time. They played games and had a barbeque. It was almost 7 o'clock when they arrived home.

As she drove the car up to the house, Rhonda thought, *The children have eaten. They are tired. I'll put them to bed. Then I'll find a frozen pizza in the freezer. I'll cook it for Kris.*

When they walked into the house, she could not believe her eyes. Kris was like a mad man. He was taking everything from the bedroom that belonged to Libby and throwing it into the living room.

"What are you doing?" Rhonda asked.

Kris didn't answer. He was taking shoes out of the closet.

"Kris! Stop! Libby will want her clothes and shoes when she comes back!" shouted Rhonda.

Rebecca was upset. "What is Daddy doing? Why is he throwing Mommy's clothes away?" she asked. "I'm frightened."

Rhonda looked at the children. Anders was starting to cry. *I must look after them.*

"It's OK," she said cheerfully. "Your Daddy is cleaning the house. Let's get ready for bed and I'll read you a story."

It was difficult to get the children to go to sleep. Finally at around 9 o'clock, the children were sleeping.

Rhonda found Kris sitting in the bedroom. "What are you doing?"

"I'm taking Libby out of my life."

"Why?"

"I talked with the new police chief today," said Kris.

"What did he say?"

"I don't want to talk about it," said Kris.

Rhonda went to the kitchen and called Damien. It was late, so he was not at work. She told the desk officer it was urgent. The desk officer knew her name and said, "OK. I will call him. He can call you."

Damien called very quickly.

"What's happening?" she asked. "Kris has gone crazy. Why?"

"Kris got bad news from my boss," said Damien.

"What bad news? Can you tell me? Can you come here?"

"OK," said Damien. "I'll be at the house in ten minutes."

"Meet me outside," said Rhonda. "I don't want Kris to know I called you."

Rhonda waited outside the house. When Damien came, she said, "We can sit in the garden."

"Please tell me. Why is Kris taking all Libby's clothes out of the bedroom?"

"I might be in trouble with my new boss, but I'll tell you. Pete contacted his friend in the FBI. He asked about Libby. He was disappointed because she didn't tell him anything. His friend said, 'There is nothing I can tell you'.

"Pete thought this was strange. So he called another friend. Finally he got an answer. This friend looked on all the databases and records. There is no person of the right age called Elizabeth Anne Emmett in any records anywhere in the USA.

"I don't know who Libby is, but Pete's friend is sure she was never called Elizabeth Anne Emmett!"

"What can we do?" asked Rhonda.

"I don't know," said Damien. "The FBI told my boss to stay away. They said, 'Don't look for her. It's not your business'."

"I understand why Kris is like a crazy man," said Rhonda. "He loved Libby so much."

"I know," said Damien. "I'm so sorry. There's nothing more that I can do."

"Thank you for coming," said Rhonda. "Thank you for telling me. I think I should go back inside now. Kris is making a lot of noise. I'm worried he will wake the children."

Damien left and she went back into the house.

Over the next few days, Kris tried to take everything that belonged to Libby out of the house. He took all her clothes to charity shops. When Rhonda asked him to stop, he shouted, "Everything about my life with Libby was a lie! I don't want any memories of her. Every time I see something that reminds me of her, I get angry."

"But maybe she'll come back," said Rhonda.

"I don't want her back. She has gone from my life and from the children's lives. I want to forget, and I want the children to forget her too."

Rhonda was worried. *I don't think Libby will come back. The children are young now, but when they are older they will ask questions. Libby was a very good mother. It's not fair. The children should have things to remember their mother.*

One day, she found Kris burning family photographs.

This is no good! I must do something.

Whenever Kris was out of the house, Rhonda looked for photographs. She took some of Libby's jewellery. She hid everything in her bedroom.

Finally Kris said, "I'm selling this house."

"What! Why?" Rhonda was shocked.

Kris' eyes filled with tears. "It's no good. Everywhere I look, something reminds me of Libby. I remember all the lies she told me." He waved his hands. "The furniture, the garden, everything…"

He sold the house and bought a townhouse on the other side of Salma. He bought new furniture. Rhonda thought the children would have a lot of trouble, but she was surprised. After a few months, they never asked about their mother. They seemed quite happy.

Kris learned to cook. He found a woman to come and clean the house and to look after the children after school.

"We're OK now," he told Rhonda. "You have done so much for us, but you need your own life. You can go back to Wilmington now."

Rhonda didn't want to go back to Wilmington because she was dating Damien. A year later, they married.

She often thought of Libby and sometimes she and Damien talked about her. But Kris never talked about her, and it seemed that the children had forgotten her too. She often saw Rebecca and Anders, but she was busy with twins of her own. Her online business was doing well, and she and Damien were very happy together.

It was four years after Libby disappeared when Kris came to see her. "I'm getting married," he said. "I've been dating a teacher from school. Her name is Beryl. Rebecca and Anders like her very much."

"Congratulations!" said Rhonda. "I'm so happy for you both."

That night, when the twins were in bed, she asked Damien, "How can Kris get married? He's still married to Libby. There was no divorce."

Damien thought about it. Then he said slowly, "The marriage wasn't legal. All the papers for the marriage said, 'Elizabeth Anne Emmett'. But that wasn't true. So I think he can marry."

CHAPTER NINE

Rhonda was helping the twins with their homework when the phone rang. It was Rebecca.

"Aunty Rhonda!" she said. "Would you and Uncle Damien like to go to Italy?"

"Italy?"

"Yes! I'm graduating from high school. I have a place at Chapel Hill. So Dad and Mom said before I go to college, we should have a special family holiday! We're going to Italy for ten days. I'm going to study languages at college and Mom has always wanted to go to Italy. We would be so happy if you and Damien and the twins could come too."

"Oh wow! It's a great idea! I'll talk to Damien when he gets home from work. I'm sure he'll say 'Yes'."

Rhonda was relaxing in a pool side chair. It was very hot. Damien was in the swimming pool with the twins. Beryl had gone shopping. She had forced Kris to go with her.

This is wonderful. I feel so relaxed. I didn't realise how tired I was. Where are Rebecca and Anders? She looked around the pool area. *There they are. They are making friends with some other young people. That's nice.*

She watched the teenagers for a while. Rebecca and Anders had grown up to be dark haired like their father. *They could be Italians,* she thought. *It's good. They don't have to be so careful in the sun.*

She looked at a group of children near the twins. *Libby had such blonde hair,* she thought. *She was slim and elegant. Rebecca looks like Kris and me. She doesn't look like Libby.*

Libby! Why am I thinking about Libby? I haven't thought about her in long time.

Then Rhonda understood. One of the younger children looked like Libby. She was maybe two years older than the twins. The young girl had long shiny blonde hair. She walked like Libby. She moved her head like Libby.

"Mom!" shouted one of twins. "I can swim underwater! Come and look!"

Rhonda forgot about the young girl who looked like Libby. She got out of her chair and went to the pool.

"OK," she smiled. "Show me what you can do."

The two families ate together on the hotel terrace. Kris was very quiet. He didn't talk or eat. After dinner he said, "Damien, can you look after the twins for a while?"

"No problem. I'll take them for a walk along the beach, before we go back to our rooms. They'll be very tired before I put them to bed."

"Anders and I are going to play beach volleyball," said Rebecca. The hotel has a court with lights! Mom said she would come and watch."

"I hope you have a good time," said Kris. He turned to Beryl. "Is that OK? I want to talk to Rhonda for a while."

Beryl smiled. "Sure. Where will you and Rhonda go?"

"We'll go to the garden bar here at the hotel," said Kris.

They walked through to the garden bar. Kris ordered drinks. He chose a table at the edge of the bar. There were not so many people nearby.

They sat with their drinks in silence for a few minutes. Then Rhonda asked, "What do you want to talk about?"

Kris held his glass so tightly that Rhonda thought he might break it. "I saw Libby today!"

"Kris no! You didn't!"

"Rhonda, you must believe me. I saw her in the street when I was shopping with Beryl."

"Stop Kris! This is bad. It is dangerous for you to think like that. Libby is gone. It is ten years since she left. You have a new life."

While Rhonda was talking to Kris, she had a very bad feeling. A cold shiver ran up her back. *I thought about Libby for the first time in years today. I thought about her because I saw that young girl at the pool. Now Kris says he saw Libby! I must be very careful.*

"We don't know if Libby's alive," she said slowly. "Everyone has a double somewhere in the world. You saw someone who looked like Libby. But that was Libby ten years ago. You don't know what she looks like now and remember she might be dead.

"You got a shock today. But you made a mistake. You mustn't talk to anyone about it."

"You're right," said Kris. "Libby was not a real person. I don't know what her real name was. Everything she told me was a lie. I said I would forget about her, and I have."

While Kris was talking, Rhonda was thinking. *I told Kris he made a mistake. But I think he did see Libby today.*

They had another drink and talked about their vacation and the children. It was late when they walked back to their hotel rooms.

Damien and Beryl were sitting on the balcony. They were talking seriously to each other, but they stopped as Kris and Rhonda arrived.

"The twins are asleep," said Damien. "Did you have a nice time?"

"Yes, thank you,' answered Rhonda.

"Anders and Rebecca have gone to their rooms," laughed Beryl. "They found beach volleyball very difficult and tiring. But they want to try again tomorrow."

The adults said 'goodnight' and went to their own rooms.

"Damien," said Rhonda quietly. "I have something to tell you!"

"Uh," said Damien. "Beryl is a bit worried. I have something to tell you too."

"This is serious!" Rhonda wanted Damien to listen.

"OK."

She told him about the young girl in the pool. She told him about the woman Kris had seen in the street. "But it's all crazy, isn't it? It's all imagination."

Damien sat on the edge of the bed and stared at his wife.

"Maybe not. Beryl went to watch Rebecca and Anders play beach volleyball. She saw a woman standing in the shadows at the edge of the court. The woman seemed strange.

"Then Beryl understood that the woman was watching Rebecca and Anders all the time. Sometimes the floodlights caught the woman's face. Beryl was frightened. She said the woman looked 'hungry'.

"Then Anders did something good and he called out to Beryl. When Beryl looked for the woman again, she was gone.

"I guess he shouted something like, 'Look what I did Mom!'"

"Oh no!" whispered Rhonda. "What are we going to do? Can we go to the police?"

"No," said Damien. "What can we tell them? I know I'm a policeman, but I can't do anything here.

"I think we should leave. But we can't do anything tonight. Try to sleep. Tomorrow we will have to make up some kind of story. It will be a difficult day."

CHAPTER TEN

Kris couldn't sleep. It was past midnight when he gave up. He dressed and walked downstairs quietly.

He walked towards the beach. A woman appeared suddenly. "Libby!" he said. "I saw you in the street today."

"You saw me," she answered. "You saw the woman you married, but I am not Libby. I was never Libby."

"But who are you? Why did you leave us?"

"We were never meant to see each other again," she said. "I don't know why this has happened."

She pointed to a seat on the edge of the beach. "Sit down and I will tell you my story. It will be difficult for me. Please don't say anything until I have finished."

"My real name doesn't matter. When I was almost eighteen years old I saw three people killed. It was part of a war between two gangs but two innocent people in the street died. They were very unlucky. They were in the wrong place at the wrong time.

"I was very frightened, but I told the police everything I saw. I said I would speak at the trial. I said I would be a witness. Before I went to court, the family of the killers sent messages to me, to the police, and to the FBI. They said they would kill me if I spoke in court. But I wanted to do it."

"Why? You were so young!"

It was very dark, and Kris couldn't see the woman's face.

But she put her hand up. "Quiet! I asked you not to speak."

"The FBI hid me. I had bodyguards all the time. I went to court. I identified the killers. Of course they went to jail for a very long time. The family of the killers said that they would never stop looking for me. They said that when they found me, they would kill me, and everyone I loved.

"The Witness Protection Program took over. A lot of people in that programme are crooks and gangsters. But sometimes they are just normal people who get caught in a bad situation. I got a new name and new life story. They created an imaginary aunt for me. Of course, none of it was true, but it was the best way to hide me. They sent me far away from my hometown, and I could go to college. I met you.

"We had a good life. I had you and our children. I loved you and Rebecca and Anders very much. I was very happy. I almost forgot my former life. Then one night I found a note on the back door of the house. It was just two words - my real name.

"I remembered what the gang had said. They had said that when they found me, they would kill me, and everyone I loved. I was so frightened. I loved you and the children so much. I knew I had to go away.

"The Witness Protection Program always worried that the gang family might find me. So there was an escape plan. It broke my heart, but I had to be sure that you and the children were safe. So I left."

Kris was quiet for a long time. He felt different. *I have had a hard place like a rock in my heart for so long,* he thought. *But now it's gone. I understand. But I have so many questions.*

"You were so young," he said. "You lost your life. Why did you go to court as a witness? What about your mother and father?"

"I didn't tell you," she said sadly. "They were the innocent people who died in the street. That's why I had to speak."

Kris thought, *I forgive her for everything. Everything she did was out of love. It must have been so hard. It is very sad.*

"What happened after you left Salma?" he asked.

"It was very difficult. The Witness Protection people thought I would never be safe in the USA. The gang family wanted revenge. They had never stopped looking for me. If they found me one time, maybe they could find me again. So they sent me to Europe."

"And?"

"Please don't be angry. I was living in France, and I met another man. He is Italian. He owns this hotel. He is much older than me, but he is kind and we are happy. It was some kind of crazy coincidence that you came here for a vacation."

"It's OK. I understand. You were lonely for so many years of your life. I was very angry and unhappy after you left. After a few years, I met another woman. She's a nice woman. You would like her. She's a very good mother."

The woman sighed. "I saw her tonight. Rebecca and Anders were playing volleyball. Anders called her 'Mom'."

I can't believe any story could hurt so much! thought Kris. *She watched our children tonight, but she couldn't speak to them.*

He sat for a long time with the woman who was once his wife. They didn't speak.

Then Kris said, "Children? Do you and your husband have children?"

"I have a daughter. Her name is Lauretia. She's nine years old."

Kris thought about times and dates. "What!" He was excited. "She is my daughter! I must meet her! She can come to America!"

The woman put her hand on Kris' arm. "Please. My husband cannot have children. She is the light of his life. You have two of our children. Please let me and my husband have Lauretia."

Kris thought about the story. He thought about all the pain and sadness and loneliness. "Of course. I'm sorry. I promise, in the future, Rebecca and Anders will be part of your life."

"No! Tomorrow, my husband will have a problem with hotel reservations. He will offer you rooms in a much better and more expensive hotel. You will leave. You will not see me, or hear from me, again."

"Does your husband know your story?"

"No. But he loves me. He will do anything I ask him. You must never tell our children about their sister or their mother. You have a new life. Go back to your wife now. Leave tomorrow and forget about me. Forget about Lauretia."

Kris stood up and walked slowly back to the hotel buildings.

Then he started to hurry. *Beryl might wake up. She will wonder where I am.*

He left a wife and mother sitting alone on the beach as he hurried towards another wife and mother.

THANK YOU

Thank you for reading A Wife and Mother. (Word count: 12,427) We hope you enjoyed the story.

If you would like to read more graded readers, please visit our website http://www.italkyoutalk.com

Other Level 4 graded readers include
Chi-obaa and Friends
Chi-obaa and Her Town
End House (Old Secrets – Modern Mysteries Book 2)
Haversham House
Killer (Old Secrets – Modern Mysteries Book 4)
On the Run (Old Secrets – Modern Mysteries Book 3)
Return to the Valley
The Blue Lace Curtain (Old Secrets – Modern Mysteries Book 1)
The Other Sisters (Old Secrets – Modern Mysteries Book 5)
The Legacy
The Temple Treasure
The Vase
The Witches of Nakashige
Vanished Away

ABOUT THE AUTHOR

I Talk You Talk Press is an award-winning Japan-based publisher of language textbooks, graded readers and language learning/teaching resources. We won the Language Learner Literature Award in 2019 and 2020.

Our team is made up of highly experienced language teachers and translators, who have all studied at least one additional language to an advanced level.

This experience enables us to design our materials from the perspective of both the teacher and the learner. We consult with both teachers and language learners when designing our textbooks and graded readers, and test our materials extensively in the classroom before publication.

We are a fast-growing press, and currently publish graded readers for learners of English. We publish new graded readers monthly.